AGENDA 21 EXPOSED!

The Demolition of Freedom through the Green Deal
& The Great Reset

2021-2030-2050

Plandemic – Economic Crisis – Hyperinflation

Truth Leaks Books

CW00606751

Disclaimer

The Vatican Approves

Deputy director: Vatican confirmed that our vaccines developed with abortion cells are acceptable

Project Veritas, in its most recent video exposing the corona-vax scam, gets Melissa Strickler on camera, whistleblower at Pfizer. She came across emails from the company's top executives in a database agreeing that information about the use of the cells of aborted fetuses in the development of the Covid "vaccines" should be kept hidden. Strickler fears that these cells were also used in the final vaccines.

Vanessa Gelman, senior director of Worldwide Research, Development & Communications, wrote in emails to Philip Dormitzer, vice president and chief scientific officer, among others, that although these human cell lines were not directly used in the experimental 'vaccine', 'one or more cell lines with an origin that can be traced back to human fetal cells' are used in the testing laboratories.

On this, Gelman writes, "This part we tried really hard not to share unless it is strictly necessary and critical to the mission... From a corporate affairs standpoint, we want to avoid having the information about the fetal cells come out. As a reason, she gives that the risk is too high that "members of the public" will use this information "in a way we don't want.

Philip Dormitzer then wrote in an email to another employee that 'HEK293T cells (HEK = Human Embryo Kidney**), used for the IVE analysis, ultimately came from an aborted fetus. On the other hand, the Vatican's doctrinal committee has confirmed that they find it acceptable for pro-life believers to be immunized.'

Strickler confirms that in doing so Pfizer has no concern for the legally recognized religious conscientious objectors. 'They are withholding knowledge from the public by which people can decide whether to consent or not.... They are so deceptive in their emails that it almost looks like these cells are in the final vaccine. That made me not trust it.'

When FDA officials visited for verification, the windows of certain rooms were blacked out. When asked why she openly turned to Project Veritas, she replied that she felt it was the right thing to do because 'my own company doesn't want to be honest with me... I was really traumatized and sick to death of the things I saw. That's why I took a leave of absence. I do feel quite a bit afraid of what they will do to me now. But I am at peace with it. The public needs to know this, because they want to give this to children.'

Why she didn't go to Congress with this? Because her lawyers advised her to go directly to Project Veritas. 'Whistleblower lawyers (and also someone who worked at the Justice Department for 17 years) told me that some things are best leaked to the media, than doing it

3

any other way. And I think that should be made public so that people realize that they are being deceived.

She concludes to her bosses at Pfizer: 'I am just one face of many of your employees who are willing to fight this and reveal to the world what is going on. All we want is for you to be transparent, honest, and do the right thing.'

Abortion cells in vaccines previously linked to cancer, leukemia and autism

A Canadian-Chinese, reportedly advanced corona vaccine, ready to be tested on humans, contains cells from aborted human fetuses. This was discovered by Dr. Alan Moy, the founder and scientific director of the John Paul II Medical Research Institute, and also CEO of Cellular Engineering Technologies. Moreover, according to him, there are already strong indications that the Ad5-nCoV vaccine, as it is called, is not going to work anyway.

Chinese firm CanSino Biologics Inc. (CanSinoBIO) is working with the National Research Council (NRC), Canada's largest federal research and development organization, in developing the Ad5-nCoV corona vaccine. Both the NRC and CanSinoBIO said they were "proud" of the long-standing collaboration "to address global health needs.

'Draconian anti-life measures'

4

Dr. Moy delved into the documentation on this vaccine, and discovered "that it uses an adenovirus replication-defective vector, and therefore HEK293, which is a cell line from aborted fetuses. According to NRC and CanSinoBIO, the patented HEK293 abortion cells 'help advance the production process for a vaccine candidate,' and provide the world with a 'working' vaccine much faster than normal.

'I'm not jealous of the Canadians,' Moy said. 'Your government and prime minister have taken draconian anti-life measures ... this is not a good vaccine solution , whether you are pro-life or pro-choice.'

Phase 2: testing on humans

The Ad5-nCoV vaccine is being developed in China in collaboration with the Beijing Institute of Biotechnology, an institution of the Communist Party. It is said to be the world's first "phase 2" corona vaccine, meaning it is "safe" enough to be tested on humans.

Abortion cells in vaccines linked to cancer, leukemia and autism

In 2010 and 2014, independent scientific studies showed a link between cells from aborted human fetuses and an increased risk of autism and leukemia. Last year, an Italian laboratory discovered that abortion cells in a chickenpox vaccine can cause cancer.

5

Table of Contents

The Coldest Winter 2021-20222?

Intentionally created energy crisis completely explodes price of natural gas and threatens to push millions into poverty - IPCC once again completely debunked: Snow mass 250 gigatons above average since 1982

The cognitive climate dissonance in the West is taking increasingly absurd forms. In September, European leaders vowed once again that - regardless of the astronomical costs - they will quickly end CO_2 emissions to stop global warming. In contrast to this narrative, which is beginning to sound more and more like a fairy tale, is the now increasingly harsh reality of global cooling, caused by the new solar minimum and the coincidence of all historical climate cycles, with which CO_2 really has nothing at all to do. The renowned Russian meteorological center Phobos now confirms the prediction that Europe is facing an 'extremely cold winter', and that while gas prices are already through the roof during this deliberately created energy crisis.

The entire Northern Hemisphere must prepare for extreme winter weather, Phobos warns. In Russia, it seems that this will happen especially from the beginning of January. For Siberia even twice as much snow as average is expected, and for Moscow a quarter more than normal. North America, including the U.S., can prepare for a repeat after last winter's record cold (702 deaths from the cold in Texas alone) that could be even more severe.

Very severe winter in the offing

Meanwhile, with this likely very severe winter ahead, Europe is facing an increasingly severe energy crisis. The price of natural gas has risen by tens of percent, in some parts even by 250% and 500%. In several countries, factories have had to shut down part or all of their operations. In Europe - one of the two main food exporters in the world - one of the largest cash crop growers in the Westland region had to turn off the lights, which does not bode well for the stability of the food supply.

In any case, winter has started very early. The Northern Hemisphere already has 250 gigatons more snow than the 1982-2012 average, completely disproving the UN IPCC climate (nonsense) panel for the umpteenth time. The Alps have also seen a heavy load of snow; the famous Stelvio pass in Italy received a 25 centimeter pack. As a result, the ski area is already open, as are 7 other winter sports centers in Italy, Austria and Switzerland. The Stubai glacier in Austria was hit by more than 30 centimeters of snowfall, as were Hintertux and Pitztal.

According to inthesnow.com, the snowline in some areas even dropped below 1,000 meters. In the Balkans and central Italy, the mercury drops to 16 degrees below the normal average temperature at night this week. Incidentally, it is also extremely cold elsewhere on the planet: the South Pole, with an average temperature of -61.1 C., has just had its coldest winter ever measured. At the Russian base Vostok it even became -79.4 C. on October 1, also a record (for that period). Also in Australia, South Africa and large parts of South America it is very cold.

War on gas, factories must close, prices explode

The main reason why energy prices are now going through the roof is the ideological war that the European climate elite has been waging against natural gas for years, as a result of which necessary investments in infrastructure and storage have not been made or have been scaled back. The historically low gas stocks this created have now caused prices to explode by tens or even hundreds of percent, yesterday in Great Britain within hours by some 78p more to 355p per unit, well above the previous record of 120p in 2018.

Natural gas prices have risen as much as 500% this year thanks to the (in many places historically) cold winter of 2020-2021, failing 'renewable' energy sources (wind, solar) and the already mentioned deliberate step-by-step dismantling of the stable gas infrastructure. The sky-high prices already forced several plants to close or reduce their production.

This will have a major impact on the consumer prices of many products, and even on their availability. Many analysts therefore fear a disastrous winter with both energy and food shortages, possibly resulting in large numbers of victims.

We reiterate that all of this is certainly not accidental or "unforeseen," but by design. The Western climate-vaccine elite has been meticulously preparing for this crisis for years, intended to partially destroy the economy and make the population as vulnerable and dependent as possible.

By making 'fossil' fuels scarce and extremely expensive, they want to justify the monstrous freedom- and wealth-destroying climate and energy investments (the 'Green New Deal') in 'green'.

With this direct attack on our energy stability and livelihoods, they want to achieve that both citizens and companies can no longer oppose the UN's "neoliberal" but in reality anarcho-communist Agenda-2030, which is made possible by the "Great Reset" of the World Economic Forum and its political lackeys, through which this party has taken control not only of the mainstream media and judiciary, but also of the largest political party).

Will people finally wake up en masse next winter, when they freeze to death outside and inside (from an as yet unconfirmed source we have heard that the natural gas bill will be an average of 900 euros higher next year, and that's presumably without the regime's planned much higher energy tax) or get completely stuck in thick layers of snow, that the CO_2-global warming fairy tale was only invented to give a small club of globalists enormous wealth, control and power, at the expense of the freedom and well-being of the ordinary population?

World War 3 starts in Taiwan?

Will the Americans once again succeed in initiating yet another major war, perhaps WW3?

Officials in Washington, according to the Wall Street Journal, have openly admitted that American special forces have been in Taiwan for at least a year to provide training, among other things. We have written many times that the possible presence of U.S. military forces on the island is an extreme provocation that could be construed by China as a casus belli, or immediate cause for war. The Chinese state-run newspaper Global Times, mouthpiece of the Communist Party (CCP) even writes that World War III could erupt "any day now.

In 1962, the Soviet Union sent troops and missiles to Cuba, which is a similar distance from the U.S. as Taiwan is from mainland China. The Americans reacted like a wasp and threatened World War III, which was only narrowly averted. What the Soviets did just under 60 years ago, the Americans are now doing themselves on Taiwan, targeting China.

Why only two dozen members? Why secret? The US should openly send 240 soldiers, in uniform, and make it known where they are stationed. Just see if the PLA then launches a targeted airstrike to destroy these U.S. invaders!' is the telling response from Hu Xijin (Chinese state media).

Taiwan: 'China will have to pay the price'

In recent weeks, as a serious warning, the Chinese air force has entered Taiwan's defense zone numerous times, sometimes with dozens of aircraft at a time. Since last Friday, as many as 150 Chinese aircraft have violated the edges of Taiwan's airspace.

Taiwanese politicians and government officials are therefore openly talking about an impending war, and seem to be counting on U.S. military support. Defense Minister Chiu Kuo-cheng said that China "has the capabilities to attack us, but will have to pay the price. He added that that price will be "lower" in 2025, as China would then be able to conduct a "full-scale invasion.

Will the Americans succeed again in triggering a massacre?

According to the Global Times, the secret cooperation between America and Taiwan has become so 'brazen' that there is almost no room left for a diplomatic solution, and a direct military confrontation has become almost inevitable. As a result, World War III "could break out at any time," it is written. Chinese media and politicians have repeatedly warned in recent years that U.S. troops on Taiwan means a red line that will be an immediate reason to start a war.

Will Washington, for so long the scourge of this planet, again succeed in setting in motion yet another great slaughter?

Our Computers Spy On Us?

IT analyst: 'You will soon not be able to run, open, play and read anything without permission from Microsoft'

Life's better together" is how Microsoft is promoting the update to Windows 11 that was officially released yesterday. Remove that 'together' quickly, because with this updated operating system Microsoft actually takes away all forms of privacy and control over your own PC. Windows-11 enables Microsoft to determine which programs you may and may not install on your PC, which files you may access, which music you may share, and even which e-mails you may read. From now on, Microsoft WILL not only SEE and record EVERYTHING you do, but it can - and will - determine your behavior in an increasingly coercive manner.

Microsoft has a long and dubious history with the step-by-step destruction of the freedom and autonomy of Windows users. For years, the company has refused to give users full insight into what the software actually does and what information is collected. Better yet, where, when and how it spies on you without your knowledge.

'Spying' may sound excessive to some, but Windows-11 requires a previously optional Microsoft account. Every user account is linked to it, so Microsoft can link your complete PC behavior to you personal identity.

Trust" is being changed to "Treachery.

Even people who use the old naive argument that "I have nothing to hide" (but meanwhile lock the doors of their cars and homes, and would certainly not be happy if their conversations were secretly monitored with hidden microphones) should now ask themselves whether it is such a good idea to automatically share all their personal files and computer activities with a company with such a dubious reputation for privacy protection and digital abuse.

However, thousands of PCs - including very recent ones - are proving to be unsuitable for the upgrade to Windows-11. In their Update window, they see the message "This PC does not currently meet all system requirements for Windows 11.

What is that system requirement? A small dedicated (also virtual) chip on the motherboard called TPM, 'Trusted Platform Module'. If TPM is controlled by the user of this PC, then it can be used for stronger encryption and privacy protection. However, in the hands of Microsoft, this 'Trust' seems to be changed to 'Treachery', or deception, betrayal.

'Microsoft may start determining which documents you are allowed to open'

It is expected that Microsoft will use this greater control to impose even stricter DRM (Digital Restrictions

16

Management) on apps and media on your PC, so that soon you will not be able to run, open or play anything without permission from Microsoft. Your "personal" computer will no longer exist from then on; instead, your PC will no longer obey you, but Microsoft.

'If Microsoft or the government doesn't like what you write in a document, they can issue new rules instructing computers not to open that document. Every computer that loads these new instructions would obey them. And thus, in Orwellian fashion, your document would retroactively disappear. You wouldn't even be able to read it yourself," warns analyst Richard Stallman at GNU.org.

'It's bitterly ironic that Microsoft calls the program that determines whether your PC is suitable for Windows-11 a "PC health check,"' comments the 36-year-old Free Software Foundation. We counter that a healthy PC respects the user's wishes, runs free software, and does not deliberately restrict the user with insidious methods (lett. computing). Such a PC would also never send the user's encryption keys back to the company's top bosses.' With Windows-11, however, all users are forced to do so.

Choose digital freedom and self-determination

'No program that you are not allowed to copy, modify or share can bring people 'together' in the way Microsoft claims. Fortunately, just around the corner, there is a real community of users that you and your loved ones can join. What you can do? Decide to stop using Windows and help a friend install GNU/Linux. In doing so, you will send Microsoft a powerful message that the subjugation of their users should have no place in Windows.'

'You may choose to replace Windows with an operating system built from free software such as Trisquel, or other versions of the GNU/Linux operating system. If you have any problems or advice to help others with this, we hope you will give us feedback on our freedom ladder campaign.'

'We hope you will take the opportunity for a big change by choosing software that nurtures community and collaboration, rather than restrictions. Let's stop falling into the trap of short-term superficial improvements of proprietary software that seems to make life better, and instead choose free software, the only software that supports the best versions of ourselves,' concludes the Free Software Foundation.

Privacy? Then Linux

'In 2030 you'll own nothing and be happy' reads an infamous slogan of Klaus 'Great Reset' Schwab's WEF. With Windows-11 a giant step is taken towards this by removing all forms of privacy and (almost) all control over your own PC. If it continues like this, not 2030 but 2025 will be the year where you own absolutely NOTHING anymore that is not under total control of the government and Big Tech.

For people who still value the term "private" and want to decide for themselves what kind of music they share, what they write in an email or what kind of websites they visit, and don't want any secret Microsoft prying eyes, there is only one thing to do: Throw Windows in the trash and switch to GNU/Linux. (As long as it is not forbidden by our increasingly authoritarian governments).

Despite years of development, the free, stable and safe Linux still has a major drawback: not all existing software programs run (well) on it. It is possible that the developers of Linux will be able to solve these problems in the next 2, 3 years, so that Linux will finally become a fully-fledged alternative for everyone. For people who only use their PC for surfing the Internet, e-mailing and light word processing, Linux Mint is already a fine (and in fact already the better) choice. If you use a lot of other programs, it's a matter of trying it out.

Still until 2025

Microsoft is still offering updates and support for Windows-10 until at least 2025, although it has to be questioned to what extent the guarantees of this unreliable company are still worth something. At least on Tweakers.net there is a step-by-step plan to bypass the system requirements of Windows-11 (including the hated mandatory Microsoft account, for me personally a breaking point). However, this may cause an unstable and possibly non-functioning system.

It's waiting for the predictable official statements and denials from Microsoft along the lines of "it's for your own security, and we really, really won't abuse this for us unlimited access to your PC. You can trust us. Really.'

The Next Plandemic Scam?

In 2009, the Wall Street Journal reported on a meeting of top billionaires such as Bill Gates, Warren Buffett, David Rockefeller, George Soros, Ted Turner, Michael Bloomberg and Oprah Winfrey, who at the time were still quite openly advocating for the substantial reduction of the world's population. In the years that followed, Gates pointed out during public lectures what he thought was the perfect method to remove billions of "unnecessary" people from this planet: vaccines. By now it is 2021 and these elitists who feel themselves to be high above the rest and above every law and morality seem to have actually begun their planned mass depopulation of the planet. A manager at an Irish university hospital warns in a video that the "vaccines" for the next planned pandemic (already announced by Gates last year) are already ready, and will kill billions of people.

Engineer Kieran Morrissey, 61, has been working at a major university hospital in Dublin for 22 years. 'There I have gained extensive knowledge of the Irish health system.' He begins by saying that he has never been anti-vax, and has always taken the well-known and mandatory injections.

Daughter with severe immune disorder due to HPV vaccine

21

Ten years ago, his daughter developed a severe autoimmune disorder after receiving the HPV vaccine Gardasil. He admits that he was then paid hush money in the form of medical status and special treatments for his daughter that she would not normally be entitled to.

Two years ago she was transferred to the adult hospital. The consulting physician there was very pleased with her blood count and overall condition, and attributed that to the medications she was taking. Then his daughter acknowledged that she had not been taking them for a year. Since she stopped taking them "she is very healthy and has no problems.

Morrissey then began to doubt the usefulness of vaccines. He stopped getting the flu vaccine. 'Since then I haven't had the flu at all.'

'Vaccines contaminate with heavy metals and cause disease'

'During my recent research into immunology and virology to better understand what's going on with these viruses and the vaccines they impose, I discovered a paper from January 2017' on nanoparticle-contaminated vaccines. The scientists in question tested 44 different vaccines since 2004. 'They found that these vaccines were contaminated with inorganic nanoparticles, including particles of heavy metals (such as aluminum, lead and iron).'

'This led me to believe that vaccines have been responsible for immune reactions for years that may manifest as influenza and other diseases. The more symptoms of these diseases, the more vaccines are given to try to prevent them. This strikes me as a kind of endless spiral between vaccines and diseases. Vaccines cause diseases, and diseases elicit even more vaccines. This is something we really need to investigate very carefully.'

'During my research, I discovered something even more disturbing. In April, Bill Gates / GAVI published an article on their website stating that Marburg will be the next major pandemic. Marburg is a relatively rare hemorrhagic fever (= with bleeding). In 2005, there were only 16 cases. What do Bill Gates and GAVI know that we don't? Why should this be a threat? Why do WHO and the mainstream media publish articles about this rare disease?'

The next (fake) PCR test is already ready

'I discovered that they have even already developed a PCR test for it. This is very disturbing, because now they can 'prove' with this test just like with Covid that anyone can have Marburg. Just like with the current PCR test for Covid, that will be hard to disprove'

Morrissey also came across papers claiming that Marburg is spread asymptomatically by bats, something that was debunked during the Covid pandemic. If you don't have symptoms, you don't have a (contagious) virus, and therefore you can't spread it asymptomatically. There is no such thing as asymptomatic spread of a virus. That's now accepted. Yet they have published papers claiming the opposite.'

RiVax vaccine contains ricin

'The biggest concerns I have are about the rapid development of a vaccine for Marburg called RiVax. This contains ricin, a toxic substance that was used in the Tokyo subway terror attack that killed a large number of people.' Ricin is a toxic protein that can cause breathing difficulties and eventually death. 'Why do they put something so dangerous in a vaccine? This is very strange, eccentric and worrying,' especially in light of the pathogenic spike protein, the most dangerous part of the SARS-CoV-2 virus, now being produced in the bodies of billions of vaxxers.

The manufacturer of RiVax claims that they have stripped ricin of its toxicity. At the same time, it also maintains that aluminum is a "safe" additive in vaccines, even though numerous studies have long questioned this. Aluminum, for example, has been linked for decades to metabolic disorders and kidney and brain disorders such as Alzheimer's disease.

'Bleeding and blood clots from Covid shots, but Marburg gets the blame'

24

'How would they start this pandemic?" continues Morrissey. 'How do they spread Marburg? Very simply, they've already started it. The vaccine damage we're seeing now from the Covid injections includes bleeding and blood clots. That is very similar to hemorrhagic fever.

Pfizer Scams the Industry?

Top biochemist Pfizer: 'I work for an evil company that now runs on Covid money' - 'We were instilled with not talking to anyone about this' - Facebook outage dress rehearsal of false flag cyber attack?

The renowned, never-before-discredited team of investigative journalists at Project Veritas put online Part 4 of a series of videos exposing the corona pandemic with its useless, even dangerous 'vaccinations'. Pfizer scientists candidly admit that the antibodies of everyone's natural immune system are better than their own 'vaccines'.

Nick Karl is an experienced biochemist at Pfizer, and has built a career in the pharmaceutical industry. Karl admits to the undercover PV journalist that those who have had Covid have stronger immunity than those who have had the Pfizer shots.

Karl: "If someone has natural immunity, if they've had Covid, then they probably have better - not better, but more antibodies to the virus. Because what the vaccine is, as I said, is that (spike) protein - that's it's just the outside. That's just one antibody against one specific part of the virus.'

This is what, for example, Dutch professor (em.) of immunology Pierre Capel has been shouting since last year, but which no one in the government and media wanted to listen to. (Still doesn't, and that's because, as you know, a whole other agenda is being carried out).

Karl: "If you actually get the virus, you're going to produce antibodies against multiple parts of the virus. And not just that outer piece, but the inner part, the actual virus. So your antibodies are probably better than the vaccination in that respect.'

'They make unvaccinated people as uncomfortable as possible'

'I have specifically.... oh no, I have signed NDAs (non-disclosure agreements) for this.'

'For example, the city needs vax passes and such. The point is to make it so uncomfortable for unvaccinated people that at some point they say 'oh what the heck, I'll just take the (vaccine).' Get it?

PV journalist: 'What do you mean?'

Karl: 'Well, if you restrict unvaccinated people from doing anything at all, and let vaccinated people do what they want, then eventually they will get vaccinated.'

Scientist Croce: 'I work for an evil company that now runs on Covid money'

Two other Pfizer scientists confirm this.

PV journalist: 'I've had Covid, and have giga immunity after 8 months. I had antibodies checked last month.'

Croce 'No problem. Same with my brother.'

PV journalist: 'Do I have to take the vaccine then?'

Croce: 'Wait... until your immunity drops.'

PV journalist: 'So I'm well protected (now that I've recovered from Covid)?'

Chris Croce, senior associate scientist at Pfizer: 'Yes.'

PV journalist: 'As much as the vaccine?'

Croce: 'Probably more.'

PV journalist: 'Why, how much more than?'

Croce: 'You are very likely protected longer because there was a natural (immune) reaction.'

Croce then admits that 'Delta' is not really the cause of the increasing number of sick, but the decreasing number of antibodies in the vaccinated.

'I mean I still feel like I work for an evil company. They try to track everyone who is vaccinated versus how many people are actually reported... In fact, our organization now runs on Covid money. You don't talk about anything that could incriminate you or Big Pharma. Even when you close the door of your office, you wonder who is listening in.'

'There are several companies to which a huge load of money was just given to produce vaccines and push them through.' When asked, for example, what happens to other treatments (such as with antibodies), he replied: 'They are pushed aside.'

PV journalist: 'Why?'

'Money. It's disgusting.'

'They're trying to get their numbers (vaccinated people), but you still shouldn't have to prove anything (vaxpas etc.). In my opinion, this is a violation of the health/privacy law. No one has the right to ask you if you are vaccinated. That's an invasion of your privacy, and I couldn't agree more.'

Pfizer scientist Khandke: 'We were instilled with not talking about this'

Pfizer scientist Rahul Khandke: 'We were instilled that the vaccine is better than you get Covid. You can't talk about this ... it's not public. You have no idea how many seminars we had to attend about this. For hours we had to hear that we were not allowed to talk about this with other people.'

'If you've built up antibodies, you should be able to prove it. It's not that crazy.'

Facebook outage dress rehearsal of false flag cyber attack WEF?

Revelations such as these bring ever closer the false flag cyber attack of the WEF, among others, which we have been warning about regularly since last year. Given the rapidly growing global awareness of the gigantic and criminal corona/Covid/vax deception of the political and Pharma elite, they may see shutting down the Internet as their only option to stop that process and stay in power a little longer. It is therefore quite conceivable that yesterday's failure of Facebook and Whatsapp was a kind of dress rehearsal.

DNA Deformation?

'This is not a vaccine. This is gene alteration' - Also horribly deformed babies born in US (2,000 official miscarriages - almost as many as from all other vaccines over the past 30+ years added together - but injections still recommended for pregnant women)

Turkish TV channel Beyaz attended a press conference where photos were shown of babies who came into the world horribly deformed after their mothers were injected with Pfizer and Moderna's Covid 'vaccines'. 'Children have been born with one eye and one tail. This is not a vaccine. This is gene alteration,' declared the chairman of the Turkish Welfare Party (Refah), Fatih Erbakan, who was accompanied by three doctors.

Pictures of children with multiple arms and legs, or with one eye, or with a completely affected body covered in hair. Erbakan: 'This is not a real vaccine. This is genetic engineering!' He shows a photograph. 'Here you see a baby born with a tail, a genetic defect. Here a baby with the skin of an animal. Here a baby with four legs and three arms... Scientifically this is called gene therapy.'

Erbakan was supported by clinical doctors, including specialist professor of neurosurgery Dr Serhat Findikli. 'This technology can also be used therapeutically, but it has a different structure and causes mutations, like babies with tails, with four legs and three arms. It is a weapon.'

31

The Ministry of Health in Japan recently confirmed that foreign substances were found in the "vaccines. 1.6 million doses of the Moderna 'injection were found to be contaminated with an unknown magnetic (nanotech) substance, which have also been found in Pfizer / BioNTech and J&J shots in the US, Spain and Germany.

The opposition leader has discussed the documents proving his claims with scientists, the station continues. Erbakan says he wants to share these proofs "with 83 million (Turks). 'Let's face these facts. Let's be honest. We have evidence and countless documents.'

US: Unprecedented number of miscarriages, but injecting pregnancies continues

In the United States, the VAERS database officially records 1969 miscarriages as a result of Covid injections. That's almost as many in just 10 months as the 2183 miscarriages in the previous 30+ years from all other vaccines combined. Despite this, the CDC advises pregnant women to just take these injections because they are said to be "safe.

Statistical expert Dr. Jessica Rose recently analyzed the VAERS database, and concluded that the numbers reported in the media need to be multiplied by 41 times to get the real numbers. That would mean that the real number of American women who have suffered miscarriages thanks to a Covid "vaccine" is already over 80,000.

One of the victims is Alexandra Lagile, who in March responded enthusiastically on her Facebook to 'preliminary' scientific studies claiming that the Covid injections are safe, and mothers pass the antibodies formed to their babies through the blood in the umbilical cord and breast milk.

Dr. Sara Beltrán Ponce (radiation oncology training) tweeted on January 28 that she was 14 weeks pregnant and "fully vaccinated" from that day forward. A few days later, she suffered a miscarriage. On social media, she made no connection with her injection, as it would have most likely meant the end of her career as a doctor.

Joseph Mengele would imagine himself in paradise in 2021

In political The Hague and the mainstream media, people put their fingers in their ears as soon as anyone makes any comparison with the 1930s and 1940s. And perhaps that comparison does indeed sell the Nazis short. After all, Dr. Joseph Mengele would have thought himself in a veritable paradise if he had lived today. His experiments on people had to be done behind barbed wire, in secret as much as possible, and only on members of minority groups such as Jews, Gypsies and homosexuals who had been stripped of all their humanity.

But now? Barbed wire is no longer necessary, for now all humans have been declared in advance to be "Untermenschen," living beings skillfully stripped of every spirituality and higher form of consciousness. All people seem to have been reduced to animals in which experimental substances may be injected at will, with horrific consequences all over the world.

These experiments are also supported, promoted and forcibly imposed by the ruling political elite, which, especially in the West, is fully supported by a mainstream media where every form of critical journalism has been banned, and which declares everything that deviates from the narrative of the elite to be a 'wacky conspiracy theory', no matter how much evidence there is for it.

(So in Turkey, despite a number of jailed journalists, there seems to be more press freedom than here, where the established press seems completely corrupted. Authentic journalists have had to resort to the alternative free media, because in the mainstream media any criticism is banned and replaced by unadulterated government (lie) propaganda).

Is the spirit now gripping humanity the most evil ever?

In 1946, World War II had claimed a total of some 70 to 85 million lives. Now the number of victims could well be many times that, since several billion people - even children and pregnant women - are already participating in this medical experiment with their health and lives. Many of them have been so brainwashed that, regardless of the permanent or even fatal damage to their own health or that of their loved ones that regularly occurs almost immediately, they continue to refuse unreservedly to blame the "vaccine". Worse, many of these people demand that everyone else be forced to be injected as well.

My own conclusion, then, is that the spirit that has now taken hold of the vast majority of humanity is darker and more diabolical than the spirit that initiated World War II and the Holocaust 80 to 90 years ago, and may even be the most evil in all of human history ever because the most horrible things are now considered "normal" (light is called darkness, and darkness is called light).

The next few years will show whether this assessment was grossly exaggerated, or was actually close to the truth. Personally, I am still very much hoping for the former.

Government Manipulation?

This is how government and media manipulate the numbers: Newly vaccinated people who need to be hospitalized are counted as 'unvaccinated'

What critical scientists and other experts have been warning about all year now seems to have become reality. A special A.I. directed project of the U.S. Department of Defense has analyzed the data of 5.6 million people over 65. Not only does it confirm that the supposed efficacy of the Covid 'vaccines' disappears after only a few months, but it also shows that vaxxers have become much more vulnerable, and the dreaded ADE (Antibody Dependant Enhancement) wave has begun among them. Indeed, the vast majority of people requiring hospitalization are fully injected.

The figures from the A.I.-driven "Project Salus," which the Ministry of Defense is carrying out in cooperation with the JAIC (Joint Artificial Intelligence Center), are frankly alarming, and shatter the fairy tale also proclaimed by European politicians that there is a "pandemic of unvaccinated people. More and more fully vaccinated people are becoming seriously ill every week.

This fits the pattern of the predicted ADE reactions, which are caused precisely by the 'vaccines' because they demonstrably make the human immune system more vulnerable, something that both the journal

Journal of Infection, the eminent vaccine expert Dr. Geert Vanden Bossche and also Erasmus and Radbouw researchers warned about in the summer.

Vaccinations rekindle p(l)andemic outbreak

The data show that the supposed efficacy of the injections starts to disappear after a period of only 2.5 to 6 months (as predicted by the prestigious MIT in May 2020 and recently confirmed by the University College London) and that the p(l)andemic outbreak is revived and accelerated precisely because of the 'vaccines'. On August 7, about 60% of those 65 and older who were hospitalized with the 'Delta' variant were fully 'vaccinated'. Two weeks later, that percentage had already risen to 71%. Many of them end up in the ICU.

Both the Pfizer and Moderna 'vaccines' - by far the most widely used - show the same pattern of a rapidly increasing number of 'breakthrough' infections (= 'vaccination' failure). The statistics are inexorable: both injections are causing more and more sick people. On August 21, 71% of new 'Covid' cases in the hospital were these types of 'breakthrough' infections.

Newly vaccinated sick people are counted among 'unvaccinated'

Bear in mind that the document acknowledges that 'vaccinated' people are only counted as such two weeks after their injections. This means that people who end up in hospital within 0 to 14 days as a result of their 'vaccination' will be counted as 'unvaccinated' in the statistics. This manipulative and misleading method of calculation, presumably also used in Europe, is designed to conceal from the public the disaster these injections are causing, so that false blame can be placed on 'unvaccinated' people.

This implies that the percentage of 'fully vaccinated' Covid sick and dead is substantially higher than 71%, and is probably more likely to be 80% or 90%. Because of the false registration method described, an exact figure cannot be stated, but a recent broadcast by the Israeli TV station Kann News found, based on government statistics, that 94% of those over 60 who now receive Covid are fully vaccinated.

Minorities especially vulnerable; Natural resistance many times more effective

A possible explanation for the fact that in the U.S. especially injected Native Americans (+50%), Hispanics (+40%) and blacks (+25%) are at substantially increased risk is that they have a higher number of ACE2 receptors in their organs. Some analysts therefore believe that the spike protein as produced by the Covid gene therapy injections is a eugenic bioweapon designed to thin out certain minorities in particular (among black Americans, the greatest resistance to the Covid injections is prevalent).

Other factors that make vaccinated people more likely to end up in the hospital are obesity, kidney failure (ESRD), chronic liver disease, and people receiving chemotherapy.

The data also show that people who have built up natural resistance after a corona infection have a significantly lower risk of ending up in the hospital. This confirms scientific studies such as the recent one in Israel that natural immunity without "vaccination" provides 13 to 27 times better protection.

How many more victims will these injections cause?

But even if the vax pass and injections were to be scrapped anyway, it will be too late for many. After all, most people have already received their injections, and now that the dreaded ADE wave seems to have started even according to this official analysis, independent scientists and medics are holding their hearts for what will happen 9 months, 12 months and 18 months after these highly controversial experimental gene therapy injections.

Meanwhile, will doctors continue to lie to the public about the "safety" of these vaccines and the number of "Covid deaths," as they have been instructed to do in the U.S., for example? In any case, a Northern Irish doctor who revealed that even in 'her' hospital almost all the seriously ill were fully vaccinated was immediately fired.

39

That's not to mention the hundreds of thousands of victims in the West who have already suffered thrombosis (resulting in heart attacks and brain haemorrhages, among other things), nor the deaths identified by pathologists as a result of the nanotech additives found in Japan, Spain, the US and Germany in all the major 'vaccines', which can now be said, without doubt, to cause immense damage to the human immune system.

Lawyers such as Thomas Renz, Reiner Fuellmich among others, therefore believe that the manufacturers - who through blatant deceit obtained permission for their failing injections - , agencies, scientists, medics and politicians who despite all scientific facts impose these injections on the people with ever harsher and more fascistic measures should be prosecuted for proven fraud, participation in an organized crime syndicate (= the globalist climate-vaccination sect around the WHO, the WEF and GAVI/Bill Gates) and committing very serious (war) crimes against humanity, which is heading for outright genocide.

Nanoparticles?

Renowned German scientists now wonder aloud if the Covid-19 injections have opened 'Pandora's box' - 'Vaccine particles destroy organs such as liver, lungs and thyroid' - German cardiologists: Many who have had myocarditis will still die within 10 years

On September 20, a conference of pathologists and scientists from the renowned Institute of Pathology in Reutlingen, Germany, took place. There has been a great stir because of the discovery of what strongly resembles microscopic chips in the bodies of 8 people who died by Covid-19 injection. These 'chips' appear to have formed in the body AFTER injection from the injected nanoparticles, which have recently been found in ALL Covid vaccines in the US. This confirms previous investigations by various scientists and other experts, who noted under the microscope that foreign substances, objects and even organisms have been put into the Covid vaccines, which seem to be 'self-thinking' in some way and after some time begin to form structures resembling some kind of operating system.

The pathologists in question are lauded German scientists from the state Institute of Pathology. The 'very serious' results of their investigations, therefore, should be taken extremely seriously.

Metallic constituents found in Germany, Austria, USA, Japan

41

Professors Dr. Arne Kurkhardt (more than 150 subject publications; chairs in Hamburg, Bern and Tübingen, and visiting professor in Japan, the USA, Korea, Sweden, Malaysia and Turkey) and Dr. Walter Lang (leader of the Privatinstitut für Pathologie in Hannover for 25 years, among others) confirmed, after tissue analyses, the findings of Professor Dr. Peter Schirmacher, who established a direct causal link in about one third of more than 40 people who died within 2 weeks of their Covid injection.

That is, these people could be directly shown to have died as a result of the 'vaccines'. The same may be true for the other deaths, but a causal link is more difficult to prove despite high probability.

A press conference also discussed the results of an Austrian research team, which came to the same conclusions as scientists in Japan and the United States. The "vaccines" contain unexplained metallic compounds, notable for their unusual shapes.

'Population possibly at risk; immediate judicial and political action needed'

The German pathologists state that the extremely disturbing results must immediately lead to 'legal and political' action, so that the true extent of the danger to the population from the Covid-19 injections can be determined.

42

This should include looking at signs of reduced fertility and the development of cancer 'due to the genetic changes of the viral RNA' in the human body. 'A suspension of Covid-19 vaccinations should be considered.'

'Pandora's box?'

In their official paper, the professors mentioned are more explicit: 'Corona Vaccinations - Pandora's Box?" they note that several of a complete laundry list of demonstrated causes of death from the injections are very typical of a viral infection. (This again points to the question we have asked many times: is the 'VACCIN' the real virus?)

However, the already oft-discussed Covid injections-induced cardiac lesions myocarditis, epicarditis and pericarditis are 'hardly recognizable macroscopically', and are 'often misinterpreted histologically as an infarction', because a sudden 'seconds of cardiac death' may have occurred, which is hardly provable afterwards. (Thus, the actual number of victims who develop heart disease and/or die from their Covid shot is most likely many times higher.)

In this regard, they also point to a disturbing August 2020 report from German cardiologists, who warned that "many" who have had myocarditis and have now survived will still die within 10 years because their hearts have been permanently damaged.

'Vaccine' particles devastate organs

Damage due to autoimmune reactions and diseases was further found in Covid vax victims. 'Vaccine' (mRNA / nano / other) particles penetrate important organs (such as liver, lungs, thyroid glands), which are destroyed incrementally (but in some cases very quickly).

The overall immune system takes a significant (permanent) hit from the injections anyway. (As we suggested recently: the Pharma manufacturers seem to want to completely disable your immune system and replace it with their injections, of which you have to get a new one every few months if you want to survive. Or, in other words, THE business model of the millennium).

Photographs of "microchips?"; "graphene oxide?

Even more frightening are the observations and photographs of numerous foreign substances and structures found in the Covid injections, not only in Germany, but earlier in Japan, Spain and the US.

'Microchips?" the pathologists ask. 'Graphene / graphene oxide?' Unknown minerals and metals (aluminum compounds and stainless steel particles) were found anyway. (All of which could serve as superconductors for a programmable and customizable operating system.) These foreign particles have been shown to cause pulmonary embolism in some of the Covid vax deaths investigated.

Reporting of vax victims is heavily suppressed

The professor-pathologists write that death certificates without mention of any vaccination should be considered "worthless. 'Involved family members remain silent out of dismay'. (Many cannot believe that their loved ones are dead thanks to a government-promoted and imposed "vaccine. Moreover, doctors deny any connection, even if someone died only hours or minutes after the injection.)

On top of that, 'treating doctors and prosecutors are not motivated' to acknowledge and find out about the connection. 'Unmotivated' is clearly a euphemism of sorts. As in Europe, the German authorities do everything in their power to suppress and deny any connection between these injections and victims. This often involves the use of harsh penalties with far-reaching consequences for the doctors, physicians and scientists involved. As a result, autopsies are flatly refused with clock-like regularity.

The consequences: more than 26,000 Europeans already officially DEAD

The paper concludes with the former president of the German Constitutional Court, Andreas Vosskuhle, writing in an op-ed in a German newspaper that "those who do not want to be vaccinated must bear the consequences. The reaction of the professors: 'FACT: Those who want to be vaccinated must ALSO bear the consequences.'

And those consequences, as of September 25, have already meant DEATH for more than 26,000 EU citizens, and health damage for nearly 2.5 million, of which 1.17 million are serious / permanent (such as disabilities). Then we're talking only about the official EMA/EudraVigilance monitor, which historically includes only a limited percentage of the actual number of victims. A statistician-analytics expert recently made the case from the official US FDA and CDC figures that there have been at least 150,000 deaths in the US from the Pfizer vaccine alone.

The Fragezeichen behind the "Pandora's Box?", as these professor-pathologists put it in black and white, can therefore be quietly dropped. The above numbers, in my personal belief, amount to nothing less than a vaccine genocide, a 'vaxxicide' or 'Covaxide' if you will. Now that the vast majority of the population has been injected with this experimental gene therapy / nanotech, this 'Pandora's Box' has been fully opened, and it is only unclear how high the number of victims will rise in the coming years.

Remote Control Vaccines?

Dr. Carrie Madej: 'This looks like an injectable superconducting operating system'

All Covid-19 vaccines are extremely well protected worldwide and shielded from external research. Why this is being done became clear as soon as independent scientists got their hands on these 'vaccines', examined the contents and were shocked by what they saw under the (electron) microscope. An American lab recently got hold of several bottles from at least three different batches of the Moderna and Johnson&Johnson injections and examined them in detail. Conclusion: all the vials contained foreign substances such as nanoparticles and strange crystalline structures and organisms that appear to be "alive" (photo above). However, these ingredients are not mentioned in a single package insert or official document (and legally they do not have to be, since they are experiments).

According to internist Dr. Carrie Madej, who personally examined the 'vaccines' in one of 'her' labs, several colleague labs in the US also examined the injectables. All of these, however, were forced to stop doing so.

A local lab in Georgia asked Dr. Madej in July to immediately examine the contents of a vial that had been injected into at least one person. Because it had been used at the end of the day, the vial was left over. Normally this should then be thrown away, but someone managed to take this Moderna 'vaccine' and give it to the lab.

'Bright colors point to superconducting material'

Dr. Madej put the 'vaccine' under a microscope. 'We didn't add anything to it, it wasn't diluted and we didn't put human tissue in it. We just put the white light of the microscope on it. Over time, of course, it came to room temperature because it came from the freezer.'

At first, the contents appeared transparent. After about two hours, however, all kinds of bright colors suddenly appeared. 'I had never seen anything like that before. There was no chemical reaction. It turned bright blue, purple, yellow and sometimes green. After investigating, I discovered that this can happen with a superconducting material when white light is shone on it. A superconducting material like an injectable computer system.' A superconducting material - conductive to WHAT?

Free moving organism with tentacles

'We saw more and more wires forming. On some threads were small cube-like structures. I don't know what those are. There were also metallic fragments in them. Not metallic fragments that I'm familiar with; these were more exotic and translucent.'

48

Then the colors began to move to the edge of the glass. There, things began to bind themselves together and grow. It looked synthetic. There was one special 'object' or organism - I don't know what to call it - that had tentacles coming out of it. It was able to raise itself up from the glass slide.'

A stunned Stew Peters: 'It was alive? This thing was alive?

Madej hesitates. 'It... it seemed to have self-awareness. It was able to grow and move freely. All I can say is that during our medical training we have never learned anything like this, and I have never encountered anything like this in my laboratories. I have shown this to other people 'in the field,' and they don't know what it is either.

'It seemed to have some kind of self-awareness'

A colleague of hers also studied the organism and got the impression that it seemed to have some kind of self-awareness. 'As if it knows we are watching it.' She acknowledges that this was more of a feeling and her intuition, but 'it was very disturbing.'

Was it just a coincidence? Could it possibly have been only in this particular vial? 'Recently we received more vials from the same manufacturer but from different batches. We put them under the microscope in the

49

same way. We discovered another such structure with tentacles. I couldn't believe it. Over time, the same colors and threads appeared. Next time I'll make a video of it, so you can really see it move.'

'Janssen lied: there are indeed lipid nanoparticles in their 'vaccine''

'We also managed to examine the contents of a Johnson & Johnson bottle. It definitely contained a substance like graphene. By the way, all those vials contained graphene-like structures, but I'm not sure if it was really this because I don't have the capabilities to test it. But it sure looked like it.'

'In both vials there were fat-like substances, something like sticky glue, which means that a hydrogel was put in there. That means they are lying to us. Janssen is lying that there are no lipid nanoparticles (as in the Pfizer shots) in their J&J vaccine. There is. In that of J&J, colors also appeared, but they were different. They were fluorescent pastel-like colors. Again, we saw synthetic structures, although in the J&J vaccine they were more circular, ring, and spherical.'

'This is definitely spiritual warfare as well'

Peters: 'If I saw something like this in a vaccine that I was told is for our health and safety, a moving organism with tentacles, I would probably run away hard. It's

50

frightening that they're injecting this into people all over the world. And you're right: in our children.'

Madej: 'People should really start thinking now and see that this is not right, and not make decisions they will regret later. I think we all know now that something is not right in the world. To me, this is definitely on the level of spiritual warfare, especially when I see this under the microscope. If we can get more samples, then we can possibly make real-time videos of it, so people can see what we are doing and have proof. But you don't have to be a scientist to see that something like this shouldn't be injected into people and children.'

Peters: 'You were talking about some kind of injectable computer system.'

Madej: 'When all those bright colors came up, I talked to nanotech and genetic engineers. They told me that the only thing that can cause this is a white light - like on the microscope - on a superconducting material, like an injectable computer system. The electronic components become visible (some time after exposure) under white light. This happened in both the Moderna and J&J samples, and proves that they are indeed putting an operating system into people.'

'So we are getting more and more pieces of evidence in our hands. All in all, this points very clearly to the beginning of transhumanism, the beginning of controlling and spying on people, as Bill Gates is now

51

doing in West Africa. Gates/GAVI are working with Mastercard and others in a test in West Africa with Covid injections and a digital ID that is immediately their only bank account. All their medical information is downloaded into this digital program IN their body. And they said if this substance - of course that hydrogel - is in these people anyway, why don't we use that for control and preventive police surveillance as well?'

'So this is what they've been doing in West Africa since July 2020, and what they want to roll out across all developed countries once they've perfected it. They call this the Wellness Pass, or vaccine passport.'

P(l)andemic pretext for injecting transhuman control system

To inject this system into people, they first had to have a pretext, and that became the corona p(l)andemic. Any average respiratory virus was extremely inflated to scare people so much that most of them would agree to enforced and even mandatory vaccinations, thus injecting them with this transhuman operating system without their knowledge.

'I have seen these things (in the vaccines) with my own eyes, things that look like they could be used for the beginning of an A.I. (artificial intelligence) IN the human body. We know that the people in power are not trustworthy at all. They have lied to us many times, as have the manufacturers. But we no longer put up with this oppression. We choose to be children of God, right? In any case, I will not go along with it.

She reaffirms Peters' summary that these are vaccine bottles from at least three different batches from Moderna and J&J, that no contamination took place, and that no other external influences such as dilution or chemical substances were used.

Peters: "People need to understand that this is not about protecting their well-being and health. (These injections) have nothing to do with that.' Indeed. In fact, these injections are THE crucial core part of establishing the system of 'the Beast' predicted in the book of Revelation.

People who choose (albeit under immense pressure and with enormous deceptions and lies, but still a choice) to be integrated into this system with these injections (of which at least 8 more are coming in e.g. Canada), will suffer the same fate as 'the Beast', regardless of their religious beliefs, simply because they can never be released from it (just as these 'vaccines' can never be removed from your body either). I just hope then that the first two injections are not yet fatal in this regard, but Dr. Madej's new discoveries are not exactly reassuring.

In an interview in the summer of 2020, Madej concluded as follows:

'Essentially, a new species is being created, and the old species, we humans as we know us today, may be destroyed... We need to rise up against it now, for ourselves, and future generations. We have a chance if we start waking up more people.

The Real damage?

Proponents of these injections find the murder of these teens and young adults, and at least 26,000 other Europeans seemingly "necessary" in order to feel "safe" again from a supposed virus that has been shown to cause no more casualties than a mild flu.

EudraVigilance, an official EU/EMA medical monitor, reports that the four main Covid-19 injections have killed 26,041 people up to September 25, and damaged the health of nearly 2.5 million people, 1,176,130 of whom have serious and/or chronic conditions, such as disabilities. The number of official "vaccine" casualties has historically been shown to be only 1% to 10% of the actual number, but nevertheless this year exceeds everything that all other vaccines have done in 30 years combined. Yet politicians, media and other headline-grabbing people are demanding with ever harsher language and measures that everyone submit to what I believe can be called a deliberate vaccine genocide, or vaxxicide for short.

The official numbers - most likely far too low because reporting of vax casualties is made extremely difficult in all countries - say it all:

Pfizer/BioNTech 12,362 deaths - 1,054,741 with health damage

Moderna 6,907 - 306,490

AstraZeneca 5,468 - 1,008,357

Johnson&Johnson 1,304 - 78,774

20 years - dead

The Slovenian government has suspended the Janssen vaccine (Johnson&Johnson) following the death of 20-year-old student Katja Jagodic, who had herself injected because it is compulsory in order to gain access to university. She had herself injected on September 16, became ill shortly thereafter, developed (as most vaxxers will eventually, according to many experts) blood clots and thrombosis, and died yesterday in a hospital in Ljubljana.

Her father walked with a mass demonstration yesterday against the Covid pass, which is mandatory to work and even to fill up with gas. 'She wanted freedom, just like everyone else here. On September 16, she had herself vaccinated with Janssen so she would no longer be restricted by this nonsense. Now she's not here anymore. She was 20 years old.'

'When you go to a vaccination center, no one warns you about the possible complications. No one warns that the J&J vaccine is not recommended for people under 40. There are only numbers. There is only talk of percentages. My Katja was not a percentage. She was my Katja.'

56

As the protesters walked onto a highway, they were fired upon by police with water cannons. Demonstrating against this legalized vax mass murder, against the medical-fascist state terrorism that forces people to participate in it, is being dealt with harshly all over the West.

13 years - blind

In France, 13-year-old boy Yassine went blind after his Pfizer shot. He received his injection on July 17, a month after the French regime Macron decided to start injecting all children as young as 12. Yassine is not exactly the first to get thrombosis, but as far as is known he was the first to get it in his eyes.

17 years - dead

Another tragedy in France: 17-year-old Sofia, a student at Valabre Gardanne Lyceum, developed all kinds of symptoms after her Pfizer injection, but still went to school. On September 20, she became deathly ill in class and was then taken to the hospital. One day later, she died of thrombosis. Sofia also took the injection only to be able to continue to participate normally in society.

19 years - dead

Another student who is no longer alive is 19-year-old Ukrainian Volodymyr Salo. On September 13, he was injected with Pfizer at 2:30 pm. Around 8 p.m. he began to feel unwell and developed a high fever. Fifteen minutes later he suffered violent seizures. University staff administered first aid until the ambulance arrived at 8:45 pm. They tried to put him on a ventilator, but by 9 p.m. he already had no pulse. Shortly afterwards he was declared dead.

Salo's family was members of the Seventh-day Adventist Church, and strongly opposed to these mRNA and viral vector DNA injections. He therefore decided not to inform his family that he would be "vaccinated" anyway. According to his brother-in-law, he did this because he wanted to be able to go to bars normally again.

15 years - dead

In Greece, the core healthy 15 year old Elias Georgakopoulos is yet another young victim of the Pfizer injection. He received his shot on September 10, which proved fatal just 3 days later when he was found lifeless in his room. At the hospital they tried to resuscitate him, but without success.

His 31-year-old brother Nikos: 'He died because of side effects of the vaccine, but they will hide that. We will do everything we can to get answers.' Together with his father and cousin, he went to the police station, but there they were told not to say anything about the 'vaccine'. 'I don't know why they said that. Everyone in the village knows he got that vaccine.'

14 years - dead

In Ruffano, Italy, 14-year-old Moroccan girl Majda El Azrak received her second Pfizer shot on August 17. She developed severe headaches, was hospitalized on August 19, and fell into a coma a few hours later. On September 13, she died. Her parents have filed suit against the doctors who administered the injection.

A suicidal, genocidal civilization - or is there still hope?

In a normal, humane society, these injections would have been immediately permanently stopped after only a few deaths because they violate all conventions on human rights and war crimes. But not in the 21st century West, where since last year, humanity and respect for human life seem to have been buried under a thick layer of inky darkness packaged as 'light'.

A civilization that under medical pretexts allows, condones, promotes and even imposes murder of healthy people and even children by means of Apartheid and other forms of coercion, can in my conviction be called suicidal ánd genocidal, and therefore perhaps deserves nothing but the inevitable and absolute demise, which by the way is brought about by its own hand.

59

Or will we finally all say NO en masse? In any case, we are receiving hopeful signals from society. including from vaxxers. The QR Code Apartheid goes too far for many and appears to be a crucial boundary. People from whom I did not expect it immediately are now making the comparison with the 1930s themselves. In all walks of life - better late than never - more and more people are starting to wake up and oppose this 'Great Reset' - Agenda 2030 climate-vaccination coup that is being carried out against us all.

Agenda Poverty & Starvation?

Coincides with deliberately created 'Great Reset' / Agenda-2030 energy crisis - 'Green Deal' will end in nightmare of cold, disease and poverty

The temporary reversal of the Beaufort flow is normal every 5 to 7 years, but now this phenomenon has not occurred for about 17 years. A study in Nature Climate Change now confirms signs that the reversal seems imminent. This means that a gigantic amount of ice-cold water could enter the Atlantic Ocean, threatening to halt the warm Gulf Stream to Europe. This will usher in a period of extreme cold in a very short time, which together with the new solar minimum that has already begun with Global Cooling, could even usher in a new Ice Age.

'This has nothing to do with CO2/Global Warming'

According to the study published on August 5, there are increasing warning signs that the crucial Atlantic Meridional Overturning Circulation (AMOC), the Gulf Stream responsible for transporting warm water to the North Atlantic and Europe, is about to shut down. The Potsdam Institute for Climate Impact Research immediately confirmed that the Gulf Stream appears to be approaching "a critical threshold.

'That has nothing to do with you, nothing to do with Global Warming,' the commentary on the Oppenheimer

61

Ranch Project (ORP) YouTube channel reads. 'But everything with the Beaufort Gyre.' This huge spinning water stream in the Arctic Ocean 'has many times more impact on climate and sea ice than anything humans can pump into the atmosphere.' For millennia, the Beaufort Gyre has determined the amount of sea ice and the climate in the north, especially in Europe.

'Recently, something has changed. It is not something that causes Global Warming. In fact, a new Ice Age is looming.' Normally, the Beaufort Gyre temporarily reverses on average every 5.4 years, releasing ice water into the Atlantic Ocean. By now, however, that reversal has not occurred for over 17 years. In the meantime, the amount of ice-cold (fresh) water - partly from record amounts of snowfall in Russia and North America - has accumulated massively (according to a JGR Oceans study, by 2018 there had already been an increase of 6400 cubic kilometers of fresh water, 40% more than in the 1970s). "Will 2022 be the year this is released?

Climate agenda ignores cooling predicted for years

The Yale School of Environment warned back in 2017 that Europe's climate will cool sharply if the Gulf Stream shuts down. 'And this is exactly what we are witnessing now,' ORP continued. 'And remember that freshwater freezes faster than saltwater.' In the 1960s and 1970s, the Beaufort Gyre previously pushed large amounts of freshwater from the Arctic Ocean into the Atlantic Ocean, causing several severe winters, among other things. In those years, the arrival of a new Ice Age was announced in the media and in schools for a reason.

The climate agenda (called the climate-vaccination sect by us) ignores this, of course. It only wants to blame you and me for rising temperatures. There are indeed rising temperatures (on which, by the way, opinions strongly differ, because there would be a cooling for years), but (well) within the normal climate variables. Nevertheless, the A.A.A.S. (American Association for the Advancement of Science) states...that sea ice controls the climate in the Northern Hemisphere.'

We are experiencing a milder climate over the past century, which has allowed our civilization to flourish. But that much-needed mild warmth has not always been there. For example, the Barbarians who invaded the Roman Empire in the 3rd century were primarily driven by cold in the north. In the Bronze Age, northern peoples moved into the Middle East and North Africa because of cold and consequent crop failures.

'This proves that climate change exists, but is natural, and is driven by mechanisms that have NOTHING to do with you and me, or CO_2. Perhaps we are now at the tipping point. They can't keep insisting that extremely cold winters are also caused by CO_2/Global Warming... The shutdown of the Gulf Stream has nothing to do with CO_2 either.'

'Tens of millions killed by fossil fuel shutdown'

'The mainstream media and the bribed mainstream 'scientists' (from e.g. the KNMI, one of the major Global Warming hoax spreaders who continue to routinely ignore or downplay the solar minimum and cold/snow/ice records around the world), are terribly wrong. So we are talking about the IPCC' (an ideological club of selected quasi-scientists and communists who want to tear down Western civilization and establish a dictatorial UN world government).

'These people have been wrong since the 1970s with their repeated panic reports and fear tactics. None of it has come true. Everything we have been saying for half a century has turned out to be correct. What these charlatans are doing to the economy by trying to shut down fossil fuels, if the Gulf Stream shuts down, could cause tens of millions of deaths. The last time this happened it got very cold in Europe

Green' energy is already failing

Let it be crystal clear that so-called 'sustainable' or 'green' energy will then fail completely. This is already happening since September in Great Britain, while it was still warm there. Even an old coal plant had to be started up, because windmills failed completely. In Eastern and Southern Europe, the end of September was already very cold for the time of year, with even frost in parts of Macedonia and Greece. In the Northern Hemisphere there is already a huge amount of snow, and that while the 2020-2021 season already counted 500 gigatons more snow than the average since 1982, thus once again disproving the 'global warming' fairy tale.

The IPCC was so sure in 2001: 'Milder winters will reduce heavy snowstorms...' The reality? The exact opposite, but that doesn't stop this fake climate institute from happily preaching the same CO_2/warming nonsense. For example, the IPCC merely points out that spring snowmass decreased by 1.12% per decade between 1981 and 2010, but 'forgets' to report that October snowmass actually increased by 2.74% per decade:

Antarctica is also unusually cold; the famous Vostok Station measured - 75.7 degrees Celsius in September, rare low for this time of year, and also evidence that our planet is cooling. The millennial climate cycles and current solar minimum could even mark the beginning of a new Ice Age.

Deliberate breakdown of energy security

Our' leaders knew this or could and should have known this, but chose nevertheless knowingly to pump useless billions in windmills and solar panels, where precisely a strengthening of the oil and gas infrastructure, and especially investments in nuclear energy would have been highly necessary to help us through a prolonged period of extreme cold.

But maintaining our standard of living and ensuring our well-being has never been the goal - quite the contrary. Rather, 'our' elites seem to be deliberately working to severely weaken the population through an energy crisis - right now natural gas prices are exploding worldwide, LNG and crude oil are also going up dramatically, and reserves are extremely low thanks to climate 'policies' - , a food crisis and a health crisis caused by mandatory 'vaccinations'.

Great Reset coup against our standard of living and freedom in full swing

As a result, the people will no longer be able to resist the communist 'Great Reset' / Agenda-2030 coup d'état that has been in progress since 2020 (and in parts much earlier). Get your head out of the sand and open your eyes before it is too late, and face the fact that 'our' administrators and governments have turned against the common people and against our future by all means possible, putting the interests of a globalist climate-vaccinationist sect (WEF / UN / WHO / IMF / EU / GAVI / Trilateral Commission) above those of their own subjects.

There is therefore, in my personal conviction, a "soft" internal coup, as I call this seizure of power since the spring of 2020. A coup, not only against our democracy, freedom, and civil rights, but also against our economy and standard of living. Against you, me, and our (grand)children, that is.

If the majority of our people continue to deny this, then only the inevitable pain of skyrocketing energy and food prices and severe shortages in a period of extreme cold and masses of sick people will possibly be able to wake them up. Although I am afraid that many have been brainwashed to such an extent that even then they will blindly believe the propaganda of the systemic politics and mainstream media, and blame their misery on the 'emissions' of their fellow human beings, especially if they turn out to be unvaccinated.

Our once flourishing civilization, with its increasingly absurd lies and suicidal tendencies, is heading for the abyss at TGV speed, just as many previous great civilizations weakened and eventually destroyed themselves from within with deep corruption, blatant nepotism, diametric and fraudulent mismanagement, and a combination of inanity, extreme indifference and eugenic, not to mention misanthropic, measures against their own populations. This was accompanied without exception by the loss of enormous human lives and wealth. Whether this deliberately initiated crash can still be prevented depends in part on how many people can still be brought to their senses in time.

Save our Kids?

'Link between these vaccines and cancer should be kept under wraps. That could really get me in terrible trouble' - 'Under no circumstances should we have to trust anything the media says'

In Project Veritas' third Covid-19 #ExposePharma video, Justin Durrant, a scientist at Johnson & Johnson, and Brandon Schadt, a member of the company's management, are seen literally saying that "kids shouldn't take that f****ng vaccine... There are unknown consequences.

PV journalist: 'So what would you say, educate your children yourself at home or let them take the vaccine?'

Schadt: 'Honestly that I that kids shouldn't get it... It's a kid, a f****ng kid, right? Kids shouldn't get that f****ng vaccine. They're children.'

'It's terrible... It's a child, you just don't - not something that's so unknown in terms of consequences that will come later.'

PV journalist: 'So would you say we don't know those consequences?'

Schadt: 'How could we. There's nobody who got it 30 years back who can say 'hey I didn't get a third eyeball'.'

PV journalist: 'So what is this about? Money?'

Schadt: 'Politics, money...'

PV journalist: 'And you just said I shouldn't trust the media?'

Schadt: 'Why should we? Not a chance! No way, we shouldn't trust anything they say under any circumstances.'

J&J scientist: 'Do NOT take our vaccine, but I didn't say anything, did I?'

PV journalist: 'Okay, if you don't think it's necessary to vaccinate babies, why do you think they're so eager to do it anyway?'

Durrant: 'Numbers.'

The J&J scientist not only believes that children should not be vaccinated, but stressed in a text message afterwards that what he said about the link to cancer 'should stay between us. I could really get into terrible trouble over that.'

PV journalist: 'So I should tell her (my 12-year-old niece) not to take the J&J vaccine?'

Durrant (winking): 'Not taking the J&J - but I didn't tell you that, did I?'

'Unvaccinated people should be made second-class citizens'

Nevertheless, he agrees with his boss's policy of bombarding the unvaccinated into second-class citizens, thus forcing them to still get injected.

Durrant: "People only react and obey when it affects their wallet. So if you work for a big company and lose your job, you better believe you're going to have to get in line for it.... If you can't work, in my mind that's punishment enough.'

'A second-class citizen - that you can't do anything that a normal citizen can do... Make it uncomfortable for them to the point that it's a vacation. 'No, not the vacation! Then I might as well do it'. In other words, take away people's freedom, their ability to go out, to go on vacation and to travel - exactly the Apartheid that has now also begun throughout the western world.

Both Durrant and Schadt say they will under no circumstances take the vaccine from their own company.

PV journalist: "Why not?

Schadt: 'I don't know. The 60% and the blood clots they reported.' He continues that in the 13 years he has worked there, there is a private atmosphere and nothing ever comes out of scandals. Schadt gives the example of Tylenol, which 'was layered with cyanide. Something bad happened, and then they had to recall these products.'

More and more people are coming to the shocking realization that these indirectly coerced injections are among the most serious (war) crimes against humanity ever committed. They even surpass in malignity that of the Nazis, because they only experimented on the in their eyes 'wrong' people. Those in power today have turned that around, and are now saying that anyone who does NOT want to undergo these gene therapy experiments is 'wrong' and must be incrementally expelled from society.

These daily continued crimes have officially cost the lives of tens of thousands of healthy people in the West alone. Millions of children are being sacrificed without a second glance on the altar of the 21st century vaccination Baal/Moloch. The darkness in the individuals who decided and are now imposing this worldwide is unfathomable and terrifying.

71

The Great Reset will Fail?

The Great Reset is 100% certain to fail, is the conviction of the American top economist Martin Armstrong. He bases this conviction on the analytical model of his unique A.I. 'Socrates', which has proven to be astonishingly accurate so many times over for decades. We have a group of elderly people over 80 trying to take over the world and push through this Fourth Industrial Revolution. They are probably hoping for a quick advance in medicine to avoid death. The good news is that this whole attempt to redesign the world and create a future where they become immortal and stay on top will fail.'

'Yes, it will be very difficult, and yes, we will have to stand firm. The good news is that what they are proposing is totally against human nature.

'They don't even have a clue what makes an economy function. From Russia and China came no major developments that advanced human society. All the innovations came from the US and Europe. Why? Because every advance in science, technology, medicine and biology is the product of curiosity. And curiosity requires that there be FREEDOM of thought.'

'Imagination is the key'

'What makes the future bright is humanity. Imagination is the key to all our flaws. If we can't imagine what the future could be like, we can't create anything. This is why communism failed, both in China and Russia. Marx transformed "equal rights" into equal material prosperity. But someone who can play soccer well should be able to go to the top and get a higher salary, because it attracts masses of people.'

'Without imagination, there are no dreams to fulfill. Einstein saw this as curiosity, always wanting to figure out how things work. Leonardo DaVinci was curious about how the body works. He examined corpses to increase his objective knowledge. Under communism you do what you are told. Individualism is not allowed.'

'That is why Marxist theory failed, and why we are now facing the monetary collapse of the Keynesian economies (= the West). The foundation must be FREEDOM of thought, inspired by curiosity and imagination.'

'Takeover world will not succeed, window closes at end of 2022'

On the initiated Agenda-2030 'Great Reset' of Klaus Schwab (WEF), Bill Gates (WHO/GAVI) and George Soros (Open Society/EU), and all their minions in international politics: 'Their objective to rule the world is absurd. They are the dreams and fantasies of academics. They will not succeed in this. Their window for this takeover of the world will close at the end of 2022.'

73

'It is inconsistent for them to claim that the Fourth Industrial Revolution is intended to help all humanity, while simultaneously having secret meetings about how they want to depopulate the world.' (Armstrong posts a screenshot of a 2009 Wall Street Journal article with the telling headline; 'Billionaires Try to Shrink World's Population', featuring infamous names such as Bill Gates, Warren Buffett, David Rockefeller, George Soros, Ted Turner, Michael Bloomberg and Oprah Winfrey).

'In 2022-2023, according to our models, we will have panic cycles around the world such as have not occurred since the 1930s. Before that there was the period 1917-1923, with revolutions in Russia and Germany. The larger German revolution led to the monarchy, but also to similar revolutions such as the Soviet Republic, the Hungarian Revolution, and the Biennio Rosso revolution in Italy. There were many other smaller uprisings, protests and strikes that resulted from the economic losses of World War I.'

'World will NOT give up its rights, revolts are in the making'

'The world is NOT ready to give up all its rights. As soon as people start waking up and realize that Covid passports (/QR codes) are PERMANENT, a wider uprising will start like wildfire. That's why the EU wants its own EU army, so they can send Italians to crush the

Germans, etc.. They will use the natural division between the Europeans against them to stay in power.'

'The censorship and cancel culture are the same as the book burnings by the Nazis. Anything that goes against the propaganda of the state must be canceled.' In Europe, even a secretary of state is immediately fired for questioning yet another authoritarian measure (the QR Apartheid code) of the ruling regime.

Nazi book burning 1933 = dissenting opinions 'burning' 2020-2021.

'Pope Francis is now denying entry to the Vatican to anyone without a Covid passport. What happened to the teachings of Christ and standing up for the oppressed? Let he who is without sin cast the first stone, right?' (The truth is that the original teachings of Christ were almost completely raped and altered as early as the 4th century, and the Roman Catholic Church that emerged then is nothing but the collection of a series of pagan (especially Babylonian) idolatries with which to this day a strange 'god', the Demiurge (= Lucifer), is worshipped.)

'They already have plans for a continuation of Covid and the pandemic to 2025-2028,' Armstrong continued. 'Hello, time to wake up and face this, before that too is banned.'

Good news, but first 'the bitter'

It is indeed good news that the Great Reset is doomed to fail. However, I do fear that the current international and national rulers will first inflict untold casualties before their regimes collapse under the weight of their failed mechalomaniacal plans and their unprecedented crimes against humanity. We will therefore have to prepare ourselves for the very worst, most miserable and bitter period in all of history.

It is hopeful that our future leaders are already coming forward. Young people are also beginning to wake up (not the fake 'woke', which is an extremist extension of old thinking). These are the ones who will soon be allowed to build the real New World; a world where everything that is now 'Big', 'Great' and collectivist will have been definitively settled and where the well-being and maximum development of each individual will finally be central.

War Criminals?

I've written it before: personally, I think parents who allow their children to be injected are sacrificing them to the 21st century version of Baal / Moloch, or "the Beast.

'It is already known that the Covid shot is SIX times more deadly for boys than Covid-19' - 'Any doctor, teacher or health care worker who promotes the Covid shot to children should be arrested for attempted murder'

Reputations and expertise, no matter how great and widely recognized once, no longer matter since last year. Numerous top scientists, medical experts and analysts, celebrated journalists and even Nobel laureates were immediately put in the corner of 'conspiracy theorists' and 'wackos' if they dared to question the official 'corona' and 'vaccination' narrative. One of them is British physician Dr. Vernon Coleman, author of more than 100 books and bestsellers and thus the most widely read medical author in the country, who for years was put on a pedestal by numerous mainstream media outlets. He has been thrown off that pedestal since last year because of his criticism. Coleman was not deterred, and warns doctors and health care workers that injecting children with experimental Covid 'vaccines' is nothing less than aiding and abetting genocide.

Coleman, about whom we posted the article "UK's most-read medical author issues unprecedented warning about Covid vaccines" on March 15, calls his latest video "probably the most important you've ever seen, especially if you have children. In Britain and other countries, younger and younger children will soon be vaccinated against Covid, 'despite evidence that this will cause more serious harm to children than Covid itself... It is known that the Covid jab is up to SIX times more deadly for boys than Covid-19. This is a horrific risk/benefit failure.'

'For more than half a century I have studied the side effects of medications. Until 18 months ago, I was regarded by drug companies as one of the world's leading experts in the field. I was invited to give lectures to doctors, nurses and other healthcare professionals.' Since March 2020, his impressive record was suddenly changed to 'conspiracy theorist' by the media and government.

'Vaccinating children against Covid is attempted murder'

'However, I am sure that more children will die or be seriously harmed by the prick than by the disease. Even the official government experts now agree with me - albeit belatedly - that Covid-19, the new name for the flu, will become weaker and weaker, something I said over a year ago.'

'My sincere opinion is that any doctor, teacher or healthcare worker who promotes the Covid shot to children should be arrested for attempted murder. I believe that any doctor, teacher or healthcare worker who does not fully explain that this is an experimental prick, and who does not give the complete list of risks, is violating the Nuremberg Code and will go to jail.'

'Doctors and nurses will be tried as war criminals'

'In fact, I doubt that more than 1 in 10,000 of those who promote the Covid prick understand that they are imposing an experimental prick. Those who want to know what the side effects are should watch my video of December 8, 2020, and then the one of February 2, 2021, in which I said that doctors and nurses who give this vaccine will be tried as war criminals.'

He wonders why schools are pushing the injections through so quickly. 'Are they sometimes afraid that the parents will discover the facts?... It comes across to me that they are using children as weapons to kill old people. The genocide continues. So please, share this video with anyone who still has functioning brain cells.'

'It gets worse: there will also be a nasal spray flu vaccine'

'And it's not just the Covid shot. The situation is getting worse. There are plans to give children a nasal spray vaccine against the flu as well. According to the info I got from the NHS, this will be a 'live' flu vaccine with a 'live' weakened flu virus in it. It is weakened, but still 'live'. Because viruses mutate all the time, there is no guarantee that this virus won't change into a more infectious version.'

'The side effects of the nasal vaccine are potentially horrendous, and include neurological and behavioral problems. The British National Formulary says the side effects are nasal discharge and bleeding, facial edema and guillain-barré syndrome, a muscle disease that is fatal to 7.5%, with complications including breathing, heart and blood pressure problems. Recovery from this can take years. The NHS probably forgot to mention this, or it no longer fitted on their pamphlet.'

However, that official NHS pamphlet seems to be aimed mainly at the children themselves, rather than their parents, and advises that after receiving the nasal vaccine, children should 'stay away from people with damaged immune systems for two weeks. Why two weeks? That deadline probably came from the same broken computer that told the government that social distancing should be one and a half meters, a number that was completely out of whack from the start. 10 meters would have made more sense, but then it would have been difficult for Biden and Fauci to stay in the same room.'

Are children capable of judging the immune system of others?

80

Can children indeed assess how good the defenses of their parents, siblings, and other people around them are? According to the government, 12-year-old children can now know the risks and long-term consequences of experimental mRNA injections, even though they are not told about them by the people who insert the needle into their arm.

Seemingly, young children are now expected to fully understand the additional risks to them when these injections are also paired with a nasal spray flu 'vaccine'. 'How safe is this? No one knows, because this is another experiment.' Many doctors also warn that after 18 months of lockdowns, social distancing and mouthguards, the immune systems of millions of people are severely weakened.

Cole scoffs that schoolchildren will then have to write essays about this, in which they 'will have to explain how the government will attribute the extra deaths to Covid-19.' Or, as we fear, to the unvaccinated.

Previous flu nasal vaccine had ZERO effect

The "vaccines" are "presumably safer than lying on a railroad track and watching the train come in, but not as safe as NOT getting this spray sprayed up your nose. And how effective will that spray be? As recently as 2016, the CDC pulled a nasal spray flu vaccine from the market because it was only 3% effective. After 3 years of use, no positive effect had been measured. 'I know the governments and doctors in the media don't approve of the facts, but this is really a fact.'

'Now you know more about the flu spray than the school will tell your child. Now you and your child can make a more informed decision.' In this regard, he points to official U.S. government statistics that list 591 deaths from the HPV vaccine, including 25 children ages 9-12 and 101 ages 12-17. 'Why do I mention this? Because they are planning to add this 'vaccine' around the same time, in the same week or so. Bear in mind that less than 1% of all adverse events are reported to the VAERS. Therefore, the actual number will undoubtedly be much higher.'

Children are now officially nothing more than guinea pigs'

'Children are now officially nothing more than guinea pigs,' Cole observes. In short, at a time when millions of people are getting shots that do all sorts of things to your body and especially your immune system, and about which no one can say anything because this is, after all, officially an experiment, the authorities want to give children a 'live' attenuated nasal flu vaccine as well as the Covid-19 shot in about the same period.

'Even Dr. Fauci (or in our country Jaap van Dissel) can't dispute that people with weakened immune systems can be hit by this or die. There goes grandma, there goes grandpa. And I believe children will also be at risk. Again: the NHS is urging children not to get too close to people with damaged immune systems. Oh yes, it's also now confirmed that the lockdowns and lack of sunlight has weakened the immune systems of millions, making them more vulnerable to infection.'

'Never examined whether all these 'vaccines' go together'

'In addition, they are going to give the HPV vaccine to some age groups as well. Nobody has tested whether this can go together with the other 'vaccines' in the coming months and years. No one has bothered to find out what these new injections and sprays will do in conjunction with all these other 'vaccines' already routinely given to children.'

'Also, millions of people will have a hard time staying warm this winter because the idiot virtuous pseudo-scientists who believe in global warming have deliberately pushed through policies that are now causing energy prices to explode. Millions of people will thus become even more vulnerable to infection.'

'Governments and doctors trust YOUR life to most fraudulent company'

Cole sideways points out that just last year the largest Covid injection manufacturer Pfizer was fined £4.2 million by the NHS for overcharging 2600% for a drug. In the US, Pfizer was fined $2.3 billion for mispromoting their products (such as not reporting proven serious side effects) and giving kickbacks to doctors (to prescribe those failing and dangerous drugs anyway). Pfizer topped the list of most fraudulent companies in the US at least until 2020.

'Yet the governments, media and tens of thousands of doctors and celebrities want to trust this company with YOUR life. After all, they make gigantic amounts of money from this. Genocide, by the way, has always been enormously profitable. And don't forget that they will blame the extra deaths on Covid-19, which will be used as an excuse for even more shots.'

Most other pharma producers are just as bad as Pfizer, according to Cole. 'If they made socks or toasters, no one would buy anything from them. But who cares what's in the drugs doctors want to inject into your child's bodies? And am I sometimes the only one who finds it strange that pregnant women should not smoke, drink, or eat certain dairy products, but cheerfully accept an experimental injection, which no one knows what it will do to them and to their unborn baby? It's an experiment.'

'This is a propaganda war, and the truth is our weapon'

'Government ministers and their advisers claim they are 'following the science', and that I am a discredited conspiracy theorist. Well, I'd rather be demonized in this way, than have to work for any government anywhere in the world; governments that instill fear, and that act faster and faster to achieve their goals. This is a propaganda war being waged with the help of the mainstream media.'